Lights Out!

Lights Out!

Kids Talk
About Summer Camp

Edited by Eric H. Arnold
and Jeffrey Loeb
Illustrations by True Kelley

A *hole in the sock* Book

Little, Brown and Company
Boston   Toronto

First Edition

Library of Congress Cataloging in Publication Data
Main entry under title:

Lights out!

   "A Hole in the Sock book."
   Summary: Line drawings and interviews with campers introduce typical experiences at summer camp, and in a camper's words, what it's like to live away from home.
   1. Camps — Juvenile literature. [1. Camps]
I. Arnold, Eric H., 1951 –   II. Loeb, Jeffrey,
1946 –   . III. Kelley, True, ill.
GV192.2.L54   1986   796.54'2   85-173
ISBN 0-316-05184-5
ISBN 0-316-05183-7 (pbk.)

*Published simultaneously in Canada
by Little, Brown & Company (Canada) Limited*

Printed in the United States of America

For Esther Arnold
E.H.A.

To Jeremy Loeb,
My Future Summer Camper
J.L.

Contents

Acknowledgments

We had a great summer gathering material for this book. With our tape recorders and microphones in hand, we set out to tape kids at summer camps in some of the prettiest settings in the country. We were included in many camp activities and traditions, and we were invited to share meals with campers and staff.

We'd like to thank the hundreds of kids who took time out from their busy camp schedules to help make this book possible. They were honest and refreshing in their responses and not short on insight.

We are grateful to National Public Radio's nightly news and features program "All Things Considered" for continually providing Hole in the Sock with a national audience, and for being a forum where issues about kids can be heard. Thank you to Executive Producer Ted Clark and Associate Producer Peter Breslow of "All Things Considered," and to Steve Reiner, now Producer for the NBC Television Stations' News Production Unit in Washington.

A special thanks to our editor, Betsy Isele, who had the vision to see *Hole in the Sock* as a series of children's books for Little, Brown and Company. It has been working with Betsy and Stephanie Lurie that has made the many hours involved in making this book a most positive, gratifying, and fun experience. And a special thanks to Kit Ward for her time and counsel.

We at Hole in the Sock thank all the members of our Advisory Board who have supported us from the very beginning: Peggy Charren, Tom Cottle, Carolyn Hansen Tracy, Valerie Henderson, Gerald Lesser, D. Bradford Spear, Dominic Varisco, and Beth Winship.

Our personal thanks to our intrepid photographers, Micki Keno and Stephan Miller; to the Public Media Foundation, who encouraged us as independent producers; to the American Camping Association for supplying us with lists and information about camps; to Joan Dolamore and Susan Patten for typing our manuscripts, often burning the midnight oil so we could meet our deadlines; to Michael Tichnor and John Welch for their legal counsel; and to Barbara Black and Angela Johnson for equipment backup and good cheer.

Thanks to Rochelle Solomon, Elizabeth Warner, Fred Lown, Jack Flynn, Tom Jefferson, Julie Overbaugh, Bernice Lockhart, Kathy Wilson, Michael Romanos, Vicki Romanos, David Fuller, and Martha Vaughan for their unfailing encouragement.

—*Eric H. Arnold*

Thanks to my patient wife, Catherine, for keeping the home fires burning while I was "camping out".

—*Jeff Loeb*

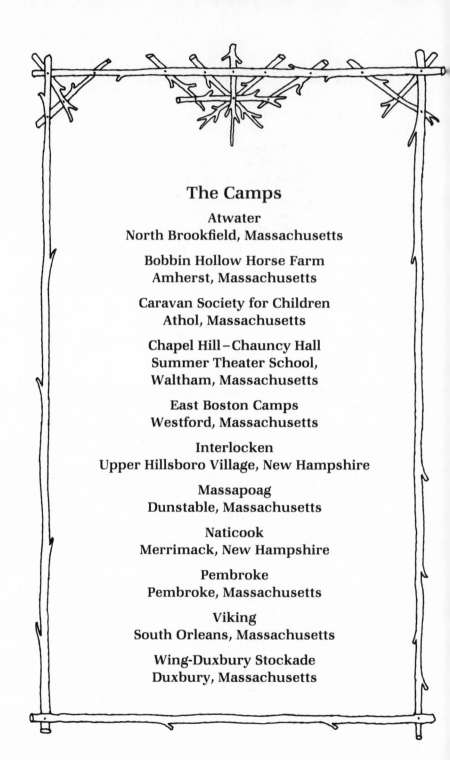

The Camps

Atwater
North Brookfield, Massachusetts

Bobbin Hollow Horse Farm
Amherst, Massachusetts

Caravan Society for Children
Athol, Massachusetts

**Chapel Hill–Chauncy Hall
Summer Theater School,
Waltham, Massachusetts**

East Boston Camps
Westford, Massachusetts

Interlocken
Upper Hillsboro Village, New Hampshire

Massapoag
Dunstable, Massachusetts

Naticook
Merrimack, New Hampshire

Pembroke
Pembroke, Massachusetts

Viking
South Orleans, Massachusetts

Wing-Duxbury Stockade
Duxbury, Massachusetts

Introduction

—Where can you have breakfast with a hundred kids every day?

—Where can you find some peace from a nagging brother or sister?

—Where can you listen to ghost stories around a blazing campfire in a pine forest?

—And where can you whisper secrets to your bunkmate late into the night?

—We found out where!

—At SUMMER CAMP!

We at Hole in the Sock went to a lot of summer camps to interview kids on tape so we could find out all about their summer camp adventures.

We discovered that there are many different kinds of overnight summer camps. There are camps for kids who like horses, and there are camps for kids who like to sail. There are camps for kids who live in the city and want to experience living in the country. Some camps specialize in sports, while others may concentrate on the arts, such as theater. It seems as if there's a camp to fit almost anyone's interest.

This book was written for you by kids your age. In their words they share with you their experiences of being away at summer camp. They talk about things like what to expect on the first day, what it's like to make friends, or how camp food compares with school food.

So if you're curious about what summer camp is like, this book might make you want to give camp a try. And if you've already decided to go away for the first time, this book can help you get ready for your first summer camp adventure. And even if it's your millionth time away at camp, this book might remind you of the fun and special times you've already had. Whatever your experience we hope you enjoy what other kids have to say about their summer camp adventures.

Lights Out!

Why I Went to Camp

"My mother . . . wanted some peace and quiet by herself."

Because it keeps me off the street and keeps me from getting in trouble.

—Jamil, 12½

My father went here years ago and he said he liked it, so I wanted to try it out.

—Jesse, 12

My mother made me go to camp because she wanted some peace and quiet by herself.

—Michael, 11

I had been to day camp before and I just thought that it would be fun to go to overnight camp, because I heard that you make a lot of new friends.

—Stephanie, 13

I decided to come to camp because I wanted to be like my sister . . . and every time we would drop her off I'd be jealous because I wanted to go but I couldn't.

—Bonnie, 12

My mother planned it, but I really wanted to get away from my brother, 'cause he's a pain.

—Darren, 10

My mother signed me up one day when I came home from school and I said I was willing to go because I never went to camp before, plus my father went to camp since he was born—not since he was born but since he was a little kid—and so he told me it was fun and all this stuff, and so I decided to come.

—Maria, 12

My parents didn't want me to go to camp; they said they'd miss me too much and I'd miss them too much and I said, "Well, I'd like to try it," and they said, "Okay." And so they write me. I get almost five or six letters from them every day.

—Ariel, 9

I had a hundred different camps to choose from, and I had very good references to them, 'cause my mom has all these books stuffed away in a closet, so it's easy for me to just go in there and pick out what camp I like, and this one sounded especially different. Everything that it said in the little booklet was so unique. And I came here for a month last year, and I really loved it, and I made so many good friends; you just become so attached to the camp in one month. It's like you've known all the people that are here since you were little, since you were small. It's interesting to see how attached you can get to some people in just one or two months.

—Kenny, 12

Everybody needs to have goals in their lives and it's hard to organize a goal when you're by yourself at home, but when you come to a camp, you're organizing something, you have projects — whether it be a play or a simple macramé thing.

—Jason, 13

All my friends have been going to camp for years; all the camps they've been to they really hated and when they came to this one, they said, "It's a great camp." And I said, "They're the experts; they've been going to different camps for four years, so if they like it, it's probably gotta be good."

—Jason, 12

Getting Ready

"We didn't pack till the night before. . . ."

This is my first year. Last year my sister came, so my mom kinda knew what we needed, except I didn't have much of the stuff, so we had to go shopping — it was a real hassle — and we had to have a list and make sure we had everything, and since we live in California, we had to drag it all out to Boston and then we had to transfer it all into a trunk, so it was a real big hassle, but after it was in the trunk, it was real easy.

—Debbie, 12

When I start packin', right, my mother wants to see what I got. Sometimes I'm so excited I put all my clothes in. My mother says, "This bag is full." She checks it. She says, "What you got all these clothes in here for?" She says, "You gonna be there about two sessions." And I say, "I don't feel like wearing my clothes twice a day." "Well," she says, "can't they wash up there?" And I say, "Yes, but I don't feel like wearing my pants twice and like that," but she says, "All right, you can bring all of your stuff, if you don't lose it." When I came back home, I lost mostly all my pants, so she told me, "This time, you're gonna pay for your clothes."

—Hayden, 13

I didn't have most of the clothes and I was so excited that we didn't pack till the night before camp started, and we'd go out and buy clothes at midnight.

—Susan, 12

Gettin' ready for camp is fun because when you put somethin' in your suitcase you think, "Oh, I'm gonna have a ball with this little doohickey thing right here," and you think about it and you put it in your suitcase—then you run upstairs and grab another toy and bring it with you, and you get to think about all the fun you're gonna have with the things you bring.

—Greg, 13

One year I came home with all of some other kid's clothing. I had some kid's underwear, size six or somethin' like that, and I had pajamas that weren't mine. My mother got really mad, 'cause I came home with no clothes, practically.

—John, 12

My mother plans like a half a week ahead and starts packing then and tells me to get my clothes ready and she washes them all. Then she tells me to find my duffel bag and all my campin' stuff and then after that, like the last night, she tells me to pack it all. It's all hectic because you're runnin' around lookin' for this and for that, and you wanna bring this certain suit or you want to bring that. So the next day you know that everything's gonna be all right, and it's all gushy and mushy 'cause your mother's cryin', or your little sister's cryin', 'cause you're leavin'. I'm thinkin' about the different things I'll be able to do, and if there's any different activities this year, or if any of the buildings will be changed—like the arts and crafts building, will it look different? What time we'll be going to bed, and who the section director will be, and all the different counselors — will they be nice? will they be mean? — and if we'll have a different boat man, or pool lady, or a different owner, or a different cook.

—Billy, 13

Saying Good-bye

"I pet my dog, kiss my parents, and split."

This is my first year up. I've been camping away from my mother and father before. Still it's hard to be away from all your little hamsters and gerbils and all your relatives.

—*David, 11*

Saying good-bye isn't really that hard. When I'm saying good-bye, I pet my dog, kiss my parents, and split. I know that I'm going to have a good time here. It's harder to say good-bye to your pets 'cause you can't tell them when you're going to be back. They don't understand. My mom tells me that when I go away my dog sleeps with her back up against my bedroom door, 'cause they keep it closed so she can't go in and chew up my socks.

—Debbie, 14

On the way to camp I was all shaky and "Oh, no, I don't want to leave and everything. I have so much stuff I wanted to do this summer. I just want to stay home. Maybe I should forget about the whole thing." When we got here I thought, "I'm free now." Your parents are sitting in your dorm and trying to get you comfortable and you're thinking you're comfortable—just leave.

—Liz, 12½

I had goin' through my mind when I was drivin' up here all the stuff I left behind. I left a lot of stuff. I left my baseball glove, and I left my pillow, and that was really goin' through my mind, 'cause I don't like to borrow things off of people. The most thing I was worried about was, I didn't tell my coach that I was leavin' to go to camp, and I can get thrown off the team, but I didn't want to tell him that I was goin' away, and I left without tellin' him that I was leavin'. It was scary because you can get in big trouble for that, because I was an all-star — I was supposed to play the all-star game.

—John, 13

First Day and Night

"You probably think you'd sleep in a gourmet bed. . . ."

When me and my mother were driving down the road I thought I was going to throw up because I was wicked nervous. It took about two days to get used to it. I've made a lot of friends. I like it.

—Ina, 12

Well, I got here and my mom unpacked me, and while I was unpacking these two girls came up and asked if I needed help. And I knew right off that they were going to be my two good friends.

—Debbie, 12

I was really scared about going to camp, and also I was kind of worried about where would I sleep. You probably think you'd sleep in a gourmet bed like you've had at home or something, but when you get to camp, you're really surprised, 'cause you sleep in a bunk with a lot of kids. Your first year is kinda the hardest, because you don't know hardly any people or anything, but you just have to find your bed, wherever you think is the best for you. This year I have a top bunk, and my friend Laurie's on the bottom bunk, which is pretty fun. We have a lot of private signals, like if she shakes the bed, that means she wants to talk to me or something.

—Andrea, 12

I live in New Jersey and I fly to camp a day early. So when I get there, I just pick the best bed and the best dresser and move the beds around and the dressers, and I pick where I want to sleep, and I find out everyone who's gonna be in my bunk. I usually pick the bed first, like near my counselors, on the right side, and then save a bed for my best friend and all the rest of the people who ask me to save them a bed.

—Jamie, 12

My first day at camp I was really nervous. I was really in the dark about what it was going to be like, since I've never really been away before. I came in by plane by myself and I was scared, 'cause they didn't tell me how I was going to be picked up or anything.

I came from Chicago O'Hare Airport to Boston, sort of a long way, and I was later than everyone else. They had to leave my luggage in the airport, which I was sort of upset about. I didn't know what I was supposed to do when I got here or anything, and I came and everyone had already eaten dinner, and I hadn't been introduced to my room-mates, or anything—everyone was just sitting talking to people they knew. After a while I started talking to people and everyone was really nice, not like, "She's new; we don't want to talk to her," and I've made a lot of friends. I really like it a lot.

—*Kim, 15*

The only thing I hate about coming back is the mosquitoes. They bite me to death!

—*Stephen, 13*

On my first day when I got here I think it should have been a fun day, and I tried to make friends with everyone. So as soon as I saw people in the hall I said "hi" and everything and introduced myself, and I got to know everyone. Like we all went down to the pool and had fun and that's how I got friends, and I love it here.

—Jessica, 14

The first day we had to take a swim test. It was the first day I had ever been in a lake. There was seaweed! Usually in a pool there's no seaweed. I got used to the lake after all the days that I swam in it.

—Jennifer, 10

It was kind of dreadful-like. You couldn't get to sleep. There were so many new things to do, you didn't know what to do first. I was confused about what to do and what not to do. I wanted to go fishing in the waterfront, but they didn't let you go down, and I didn't know what to do, so we started playing basketball and that punching-bag thing.

—Richard, 9

Well, Jamie's my best friend, and she flies in a day early, so I can always rely on her to pick out a good bed for me. And she always picks out someone for a bed next to me who she thinks I would like to sleep next to, so it's really good for me.

— Nikki, 12

I was kinda shy and didn't talk that much. Now I act like I been here for a long time. I was afraid that people would laugh at my name. At home people call me Edgar Egghead.

— Edgar, 11

This year I came last and I have a bunk bed. I'm on the bottom bed and I wake up and I hit my head on the bunk bed and, like, I really hate this. Next year I'm gonna try and come earlier, 'cause if you come earlier you get a better bed.

— Amanda, 11

Rise and Shine

"You feel muggy and you're kinda damp. . . ."

Past few days, by mistake, I've been sleepin' through the whistle and I've been wakin' up like ten minutes late. When the counselors come to wake you up, it's like, "What's the matter, is there a fire drill?"

—*Debbie, 10*

I'm usually up at five (in the morning) 'cause I go to bed by nine-thirty every night, and when I get up I can get dressed, and I make my bed, and I read my book and write all of the letters, so, like, during the day, I have all the time to myself when everybody else is busy.

—*Stephanie, 13*

If it's a really cold day, like, you feel stiff and the first thing you reach for is socks, usually, for your feet. And if it's a hot day, because you're so hot, you don't want to get out of bed, 'cause you know it's gonna be really hot out when you go outside and you'll start sweating.

—Diane, 12

I remember the first morning at camp; it was a Monday. I woke up and I forgot that I wasn't in my own bed, and I was hardly awake. I put my foot out, and then I put my other foot out and went "BOOM." I hit the ground real hard. I fell off the top bunk. The whole cabin was laughing. I was laughing too, but I was in pain. I was in serious pain.

—Bunkie, 11

In the morning, the counselors are all up at five-thirty, 'cause they have to feed the horses and everything, and then they come up at seven and wake us up. If you don't get out of bed, like, right away, they call you "P.C." and "S.C.," (Privileged Camper and Special Camper), 'n stuff. If you don't get up and you miss breakfast, you can't ride for a day.

—*Robyn, 14*

I'm usually up first in my bunk and so I wake everyone up and jump around, and I'm usually up before all the head counselors go around and wake everyone up. Last year our counselor, if you didn't get up, he'd take your whole mattress and dump it on the floor with you on it.

—*David, 10*

What it's like to get up in the morning: you feel muggy and you're kinda damp in the sleeping bag 'cause of mildew 'n stuff, so it kinda gets to you when you have to wake up so early. I think reveille is at seven o'clock, and sometimes you oversleep the bell and you can't hear it.

—John, 12

Our counselors, if you don't get up, count to three and then they jump on you and pull off the covers and everything. I'm lucky it never happened to me, but it's happened to many kids in my bunk.

—Lauren, 10½

Living Away from Home

"I miss my bird, Herman. . . ."

I don't think that it's such a big deal to get away from your parents. It's not really like living away from home for good, you know, I mean it's just for six weeks, so it's no big deal. But the thing about this camp is that the rules are *so* strict here, you cannot do anything. It's confining for me, because at home, since I have a good relationship with my parents, I can do pretty much what I want to do, and here it's just like jail.

—Henry, 15

Living away from home is good and bad. First of all I miss my bird, Herman, and my dog, Daisy, and my mother and father, but I don't miss my sister, because we don't get along very well and she's a pain. She follows me around and everything.

—Jolie, 13¾

You have to bring your sheets and towels and do your laundry and all kinds of crazy stuff, and it's really weird to have to take care of yourself, all by yourself, and have nobody take care of you.

—Chad, 14

Right before you're about to go to bed, and you're not in your own room the first couple of days, you have time to think, "Gee, wow, I'm not at home. You know, I can't call my friend who lives next door or anything." But other than that, I think it's a really neat experience.

—Kim, 15

I miss my dog, Zero, and my father, and I miss when my dog, Zero, sleeps in the bed with me and rolls up in the covers with me.

—Tammy, 9

If it weren't for the telephone, I wouldn't be able to take it. It's hard when you live away from home, especially when you're far away—your parents can't come visit you a lot. And I think staying for three weeks is a really good idea, because for your first time at camp, for your first real time away from home, it's kinda hard to stay away for a real long time. You sort of have to build up to it.

—Jill, 12

The first time I ever came to this camp, I was all homesick. I thought my mother and father were gonna move away someplace and forget about me, leavin' me at this camp. Last year I loved writing letters to my mother, and I felt like my mother was right with me.

—Aaron, 10

When I come back I appreciate my parents more and what they do for me.

—Katherine, 13

It's a lot different up in the woods, 'cause it's about forty-five miles away from the city, and up here you don't hear about fires and robberies and shootings and car theft and everything. It's quiet; it's peaceful. I really wouldn't want to live up here, though, 'stead of like in the city, 'cause I really couldn't take it up here that much. It's country life and everything. There's probably nothing to do 'round here. They have a lot of bikies up here and they drive through the camps, and that's all they do is really drive their dirt bikes.

—John, 13

Living up here at camp is a lot different. 'Cause I'm an only child, I don't share a room with anybody, and here I'm sharing it with five people. It's not weird anymore, but it was when I first came up here.

—Robert, 12

I'm at camp with my sister, and I think I get along better with her here. I see her a lot, but I'm not constantly around her. We're not getting into as many fights as we do at home.

—Marilyn, 14

You don't have the time to get homesick, because you're surrounded by so many people. Even the people you don't like become one giant family and you're busy, you're having too much fun to be homesick. Once in a while, like late at night, you'll be thinking about your home, you'll be half awake and thinking you were there. I've never, ever, in the five years that I've been here, seriously wanted to go home, 'cause I've always had such a good time here. There are always people to talk to; it's not always that way at home.

—Debbie, 14

It's like havin' a big slumber party all week long.

—Rachel, 12

It's kinda fun and kinda not, 'cause you miss your sister's naggin' you around: "Can I ride your bike? Can I make your tires flat? Can I blow 'em up? Can I pop 'em?" or "Can you braid my doll's hair? Can you ask mommy to give me a piece of cake?"

—Ronald, 11

Camp Food

"I thought we were having french flies.*"*

At the beginning of camp we had a cook named Wally, and one morning when I was having my breakfast, I found a watermelon pit in my pancake, and another time for lunch we were having hamburgers and french fries, and I found a burnt fly in my french fry, and ever since then I'm glad we got a different cook. At first I thought we were having french *flies.*

—*Allison, 11*

For lunch today the food was really good. It was American chop suey — I think that's what it was.

—*Tammy, 9½*

A lot of times when we have peanut butter and jelly, they take the peanut butter and the jelly and they, like, whip it together and then put it on the sandwich. Once it's

25

whipped together, it *does* taste different. Some people think it doesn't, but I think it's sorta gross.

—*Bonnie, 12*

I eat more at home than I do at camp, 'cause the camp food tastes, like, predigested. It's so gross.

—*Susan, 12*

I like it when the chef wears his Italiano shirt, because that means we're gonna have pizza, and the pizza's really good.

—*Lenny, 12*

Camp food is like a three-thousand-dollar restaurant compared to school food. You don't break your teeth here on little hamburgers.

—*Jason, 14½*

Making Friends

"It's like snapping your fingers."

The first day at camp, a busload of kids came to this camp, and they got off the bus and some of them were in my hut. They were unpacking, and I started saying, "Hi, what's your name?" and "Where are you from?" And I shook hands with them and said, "My name's Vincent."

—Vincent, 11

It's sort of easy making friends since everybody here is from everywhere else and you don't know anybody. You're eager to make friends with anybody. It's a different experience. People have different slangs, wear clothes differently, because we're from different areas.

—James, 12

You do everything together around here. You watch TV together, you live together, and you eat together, so it's easy to make friends.

—Lydia, 13

Making friends is the most important part of camp, so everyone really went out of their way.

—*Abigail, 15*

This is my second year here, so you just go around meeting people. It's really fun. When it's your second year, you're the one who is meeting people, you're the outgoing one.

—*Christy, 13*

I made a lot of friends this year. This is my third year, and I've made like a hundred friends. I like this camp. You can make good friends here.

—*Marc, 12*

The first day you got no time to make friends—you're doing so much stuff—except for the people in your cabin. When it comes to making friends with girls, you only get to see 'em after supper. After rest hour we go to the girl's pool for about one hour at "potpourri." It's hard to make friends the first day, especially with girls.

—*Joey, 13½*

The girls, some can be real stubborn and don't like friends except girls. They act like they're allergic to boys.

—*Mike, 12*

Making friends at camp is a lot of fun. Some of them are different colored and you can get to meet new people.

—Kim, 10

It's easy to get friends up here because they can't avoid you up here. They have to ask you your name and everything. All the other kids can't avoid you 'cause you have to go right past them.

—Kory, 13

When you're up at camp you're living with the kids in your bunk and you can't really, like, hate them. Then it's going to be like you're always off on your own. People will take sides and stuff. Our cabin has gotten into many fights, and our counselors always handled them. We sat there during rest hour and talked about it. We got it out in the open. We ended up as friends by the time rest hour was over.

—Joelle, 11

When you live with each other for a long time, you get on each other's nerves. Most of our fights are about little things. For instance, I had one the other day with my C.I.T. [Counselor in Training]. I left the curling iron on and it became a big thing. I guess that's what happens when you live with someone, just like at home.

—Heather, 14

It's like snapping your fingers. I made friends right off the bat. I said, "Hi, my name is Kenneth," and they told me their names, and then we just took a swim. We went for dinner, and lunch and stuff, and I made more friends. It's a lot easier to make friends here than home. You feel more comfortable.

—Kenny, 13

It's a very affectionate camp. At this camp we've got a ritual—"peep, peep, peeping"—and what you do is you just yell, "Peep, peep, peeping," and anyone who is within earshot is required to give the person who is peeping a hug, so it's a great thing to have. If you ever need a hug around here all you have to do is yell, "Peep, peep, peeping," and somebody will give you a hug.

—Lara, 15

It's like five minutes after your parents leave on the first day, you already have two friends.

—Lorna, 11

Making friends is one of the most difficult things. I think you can have a lot of little friends, but the best thing is to have a best friend. I am searching for a best friend.

—Marco, 14

Well, the first day we were on the bus, and I didn't know anybody, and I started talkin' to some kids. There were about two-hundred kids, and there were five buses that came down. And I was just sittin' there by myself, and I just started talking to this one kid, and I was talkin' to him the whole bus ride up. I've been in the same cabin with him ever since, and we're pretty good friends.

—*Charlie, 13*

Counselors

"Counselors are just like normal people."

Sometimes they can be really picky, like if you don't sweep the floor quick enough, you get in trouble, and if you do it too quickly, you get in trouble also.

—Jennifer, 11

The counselors here are wicked good, because they treat you like you're part of a family, and they treat you with respect. You treat them with respect and they'll do stuff for you, if you're nice to them. They're just all-around, wicked nice.

—Susie, 12

I wouldn't personally come here as a counselor, because I don't like the way that they treat the counselors. Sometimes they get down pretty hard on them, and the counselors get really uptight. They don't mean to, but sometimes they just yell at the kids. I mean, they'll apologize afterwards, but they're under a lot of pressure to organize everything for everyone, and sometimes it's really hard for them.

—Elysa, 13

I don't have any bad things to say about my counselor, Karen. She's kinda like a mother who tucks you in at night and kisses you, but then she's kinda like an older sister who you can talk about certain things with that you can't talk about with others, and she's also like a younger brother or something that you can yell at.

—Ina, 12

Well, we have a senior counselor and a counselor from Spain in our cabin, and the senior counselor acts like a drill sergeant. He's barking out orders all the time, telling us to line up straight or we won't eat, and he's filling us with discipline that we don't need. He's saying, "Attenshun!" or "Fall in" or "At ease." He was in the Marines.

—Alex, 12

Sometimes, you know, they can get in the way. Like if you're having an argument, you don't want this person to come up and say, "Hey, let's talk it out," because sometimes you really don't feel like talking it out. Sometimes you sorta want to be mad for a while and try to get it all out before you really want to make up with somebody. But there is a time when you do want to make up, 'cause I know a lot of times I really don't want to be mad with someone, and a counselor can be there to, like, break the ice and get you started to talk and work it out.

—Alanna, 13

This month my counselor is Peter. In the middle of last month, I decided I missed my brother so much that Peter was gonna become my brother and I asked him if that was okay. So now he's my brother and I'm his sister and it's just great, 'cause it's like having a home away from home.

—Lara, 15

The counselors are great — they're just like kids! They're not too rough or nothing.

—David, 11

The counselors here are very nice. It's just that sometimes they yell at you, but that's not their fault. It's our fault for bein' bad.

—Jennifer, 11

Counselors are just like normal people. You get in fights with them too. They're always there for you. They're like your parents while you're away from home.

—Heather, 14

Writing Home

"I'm having fun. Write back. Details later."

We have to write home three times a week to get into dinner so your parents know you're okay. It's not that hard to write home. You just write the news, what you do, and you tell about your activities.

—Jennie, 11

I like getting mail, and whenever I read letters from my parents, I get, like, not homesick, but I always miss them. I just like hearing about what's going on at home and stuff I'm missing and stuff I'm not missing.

—Stephanie, 13

What's fun that my parents and I just started a couple years ago, when I started to go to this camp, is that I bring tapes and my tape recorder up to camp and we send letters; we tape our voices.

—Beth, 12

We get mail at rest hour in a mailbag. If people don't get letters, they feel really bad, but, if you don't get a letter from your parents, for, like, four days or something, you get to call.

—Andrea, 12

I enjoy writing home in the beginning, but at the end it gets kind of boring. But I like receiving letters, and sometimes, because you know that you're loved at home, it gives you a good feeling.

—Debra, 10½

I write a lot of letters to home, but I keep forgettin' to mail 'em. I wrote a letter like the third day. Finally I mailed it today and what happened was, my mother called up; she said she wants me to mail letters.

—David, 11

Usually when I write my father, I answer his letters exactly. Like he's really concerned about whether I have enough clothes left or anything, so I usually have to reassure him that I have enough clothes, and I have to take allergy pills and I tell him that's going fine. But when I write my mom, it's more like I tell her personal things, you know, stuff like I can't tell my dad. Not that I don't feel comfortable with him, it's just some things my mother understands more about than my dad does.

—Alanna, 13

I think my story is very different from Alanna's. I write both my parents and I always address my letters: "Dear Mom and Dad." I don't see any reason to write them separate, because I tell them exactly the same things, and I think they both relate equally well to whatever I say.

—Susie, 13

When I write to my father, I always talk about things that I do that he'd be interested in. My father told me, "When you're in the water swimming, think about your father working all day." Then I wrote back to him sayin' that I did. It was funny. Then I wrote to my dog. I wrote, "Woof, woof." That's all I wrote in the letter was "Woof, woof."

—Sabrena, 11

My father, he's really nice. Whenever I write to him, he likes to hear what I do all day and what I do all that week. He likes it when he sees me writin' to him, because he knows that I miss him and he misses me. Every year I come up here, he usually sends me cookies.

—Marsha, 11

I've written to six friends, and I just wrote, "Dear Jenny (or whoever), I'm having fun. Write back. Details later." And that's all I wrote so they'd write. I've gotten a lot of letters, so I guess it worked.

—Ina, 12

A lot of people, before I left, they'd give me a present. They'd say, "Oh, before you go I'd like you to have something," and almost all the people gave me stationery. And I thought, "Sure, an hour of rest hour, an hour of free time, no problem." But it gets difficult after a while, because I'll

be writing, you know, ten letters nonstop. I'll thank someone for a package, and then they've sent me like ten letters
in the same day, so I'll write again 'cause I can't keep track
of what I'm writing. I'll say, "Excuse me if I've told you this
already; it's hard to keep track of what I'm writing to who,
but blah blah blah blah . . ."

—Ariel, 9

Activities

"You can't get bored. . . ."

The whole camp is mainly arranged for fun and games. They have basketball, which is arranged as a class, and you have free time for swimming and you have free time for archery and arts and crafts. The whole camp is designed to be a "fun machine" kind of thing.

—*James, 12*

My favorite thing to do here is rock climb because there are a lot of good cliffs around. It's really challenging. It's just you against the rock, it's not you against somebody else. I've learned how to "belay,"* which is really challenging, and I don't get to do that at home. That's why it's so special.

—*Jamie, 14*

* Belay: to secure a rope around a person when rock climbing or mountain climbing.

Sports here are softball, swimming, and running track. The one I like most is swimming. I got best swimmer three years in a row. This year I can't go swimming. I got on a cast.

—*Oji, 10*

There is lots of sports. You can't get bored 'cause you're not playing the same sport day after day. If you run out of games, they think of games for you to play.

—*David, 11*

Fun and games here are better than I expected them to be. The last camp I went to was a nature camp. We played a lot of nature games and they weren't that fun to me. That camp was sort of like you were in the "olden days." This camp has new games that are more modern. They have games like break-dancing competition and computers, more modern stuff. I doubt that the nature camp has break dancing.

—*Kenneth, 12*

Archery is my favorite sport because I like getting points and it happens that I get bull's-eyes. Once I got four arrows — twenty-eight points.

— *Michelle, 11*

Last year we had this great thing called "Windsor Archaeology." The counselors, before camp started, decided to make a crown and hide it somewhere around camp, but they wouldn't tell us it was a fake. They got the whole camp to believe that there was a sect run by a druid who lost his crown, and they made up a whole big paper and drew a map and spilled coffee on it to give it an old effect and hid it in different places. You had to get through bogs three-feet deep and you're all muddied up.

— *Jason, 12*

Sports is fun because we get a team and we play the counselors and the junior staff and some of the older people. We're starting a breakin' team and a track team. We fish a lot down here.

— *Michael, 13*

Sometimes when it's raining and stuff, we have horseless horse shows in the indoor rings. A horseless horse show is when from the waist up you're a rider and from the waist down you're a horse. You go and you jump and you get ribbons for it and stuff.

— *Jacki, 10*

The nice-thoughts box is, you don't put in anything that you don't like about someone; you put in something that you like about that person, like you think something is pretty about that person. We have a small fire and we read the nice thoughts, and then we burn them so the nice thoughts will go all over the place.

—Marcia, 11

The most popular sport is tetherball. Everybody, *everybody* plays tetherball, I think. Well, almost everybody.

—Bunkie, 11

The greatest thing about this camp is that they have such strange activities. That's what attracted me. I remember four years ago we had to design and write down our own superhero! The first day we talked about what would make an ideal superhero. The second day we wrote down the characteristics of our own superhero, and then we took a life-sized piece of paper and we wrote down and drew a great picture of our superhero. I had a great time doing that. My superhero is called "Dynamic Disc." He was this great guy with discs, and he would throw them and stop all the bad guys.

—*Ken, 12*

Here at camp they have all the major sports, b-ball, Frisbee, soccer, swimming, softball. They always try to get the best counselors to do the job properly. In soccer they hired this soccer player from, I think, Europe or somewhere, so they always try to get you the best in everything.

—*James, 12*

I like archery, softball, and soccer because it's fun to do. Even though I got hit in the eye with a softball, I still like it.

—*James, 11*

There's a thing called "Pandora's box." There's a whole box of candy which is hidden in a certain place with clues leading to it. Last time we had it there were thirty-two clues, and we had to find all of them and write down what the clues were and go and search for it. We found it—a whole thing of candy!!! It was in the third pasture beyond the woods. Somebody found it by accident, going to the bathroom.

—Yuko, 15

I like cooking 'cause you make a lot of different things, like angel cakes and stuffed pastry. We have snacktime after rest hour and that's when we eat it.

—Melissa, 10

Parents Day

"It looks like a stampede!"

It's kind of exciting! You can feel the tension building. Just before it's time for you to leave to see your parents, they ring a giant bell, and then they say, "Wait!" and they say, "Do you want to leave?" and you gotta keep saying, "Yes! Yes!" louder and louder, and then they say, "Ready?" and then they say, "Stop!" sometimes, and you gotta sit down. Then they say, "Go!" and everyone's running across the fields so fast, it looks like a stampede! And then when you see your parents, sometimes they start cryin' 'cause they're happy to see you, and they start askin' you all sorts of questions. It's just fun.

— Billy, 13

I miss my parents a real lot, and when I see them I get really excited. I have a little brother that comes up too. He likes to know a lot about camp, and he's gonna go in a few years. It's just fun seein' them. They give you stuff and you tell them about camp and you show them the activities. It's a happy day for you, but then at the end of the day you sorta get sad and stuff, and you look forward to seeing them when camp is over.

—Melissa, 12

On parents day, they have a lot of activities like boating, swimming in the girls' pool, swimming in the boys' pool, and you get to walk around the camp without counselors, without supervision, just walk with your parents. It's really one of the funnest days of going to camp.

—John, 12

It's kind of exciting. You almost feel proud about showin' your parents your cabin and stuff—how clean it looks— and just around the camp in general, like the pool and pond and things like that, the nature museum and everything.

—Steven, 13

When my parents came, they came before the time they were supposed to come. I just kinda strolled out to the deck to find something to do and I saw them and I was very surprised. I just ran up and gave my mom a big hug and gave her a tour of the camp. She was very impressed and so was my father. Dragging them along to the various things that were going on the schedule, sometimes you're kinda saying, "Why don't I show you my cabin now?" or "Now I'll show you the dining hall," or "Now I'll show you the deck," and it seems like you don't have enough time to show everything you want to show.

— Kenny, 12

I felt real good about seein' my parents, 'cause I think my parents are some of the neatest people around. I felt kind of strange 'cause everybody else's parents were here, and it was kinda weird meeting other people's parents, but the most fun thing was just going out with my parents and showing them the things I did and really freaking them out when I jumped off the ropes course on purpose.

— Stuart, 15

My parents went to Italy about a week after I came here, so they didn't really have time to come and see the camp. A lot of times, I really wish I could just see them once. We do a lot of things for the camp, like we made a book of the natural foods that grow around here you can eat. You know, there are a lot of times when I'll do something for the camp, and we'll finish it and I'll say, "I wish my parents could see me now." Or I'll complete a puppet or something, and so a lot of times I really wish that my parents could see what I was doing. I think that maybe, though, if I had seen my parents on visiting day, I would've really missed home a lot after they left. But it still would've been nice to see them.

—*Ariel, 9*

I know that whenever my parents come up every year, I always put on this macho look like I didn't miss them that much. "Everything's okay. Everything's fine." Oh, I was cool. Whenever my sister sees them, she always runs right up to them and hugs them and all that, and I just wait back and let them come to me. I know that when my parents come up for visiting day, we're always very nice to each other. We don't fight or anything like that. I know that I don't seem to act like myself really. I guess it takes a little time to get reacquainted with them, even though it doesn't seem like you have to get to know your parents again. I know that we tend not to be ourselves when we're together on a day when we've been away for a month. If there's a nitty-gritty fight I could pick, I don't pick it. Maybe I'm more conservative; I won't be as open as I usually am with them.

—*Jason, 13*

Campfire

"First you get bitten alive. . . ."

First you get bitten alive, but the best part of a campfire is you're usually with your friends or with the boys.

—*Rene, 12*

This year when we had a campfire, we had this sort of spook-walk planned out, and I was supposed to ride the horse I take care of up to the area where the campfire was being held and try to scare everyone. But when I got out there, he wanted to go right back to the barn, so that wasn't too easy. The thing is that nobody got scared, because I was in the back pasture running around. No one heard me and I was just sitting there. Then, finally, one of the counselors came out and got on him and rode. Most campfires we just tell a lot of ghost stories and try to learn the songs, the camp songs.

—*Liz, 15*

One of the nice things about the campfire is that even though there's a large variety of songs and everyone sings along with them, there's usually one or two songs that we sing all the time. This year the tent-unit campfire song is "American Pie," and, like, in ten years when anybody from this unit hears this song, they'll call somebody else or get sad and reminisce about camp experiences. It's just something really nice to have that everybody can go to after evening activity. It's just really cool. The last-night campfires are also really nice, 'cause everybody sings and everybody's crying; they know that they're having fun, but they're sad that they're leaving the next day.

— Lara, 15

We have quite a lot of campfires here at camp, just ones to sit around. A lot of times we have storytelling and songs. This Sunday I'm gonna be one of the storytellers, which is a lot of fun. One time we even roasted marshmallows; that was fun, and yummy too.

— Brad, 10

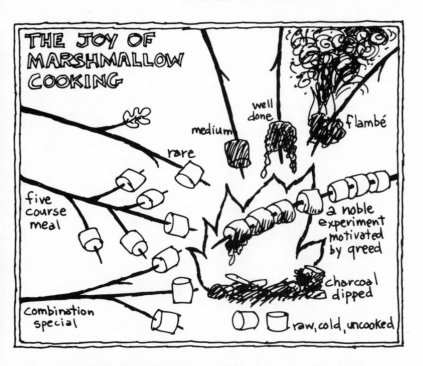

I like campfires because you can lie down in the grass. You don't have to be in your bed, and you don't have to go to sleep. There's always songs and stories and a nice fire to keep you warm.

—Zaw, 8

Sometimes when we have campfires, this man named Odds Bodkins tells stories. He's a really wonderful storyteller and he accompanies his stories with a guitar. And sometimes they're scary and sometimes they have a moral. I like to sit and listen to the stories or a song and watch the fire.

—Daniel, 12

The Funniest Thing

"Oh, slimy worms!"

We have a rooster here that wakes up in the morning, and it didn't know how to cockadoodledoo until recently. It used to sound like a dying donkey, and it'd go "ahhhhh . . ." or "grooooaaaan," and it was absolutely terrible to wake up to.

—Daniel, 12

The funniest bad thing I've ever done was put shaving cream in somebody's shoes. When they put their feet in they go, "Oh, slimy worms!"

—Christopher, 11

The funniest thing that ever happened at camp was last summer at the end of the first month. One of the kids in the tent unit, John, had a very difficult time getting up in the morning. So finally, about four people from the tent unit, including the counselors, while he was sleeping in his underwear under his mosquito net, lifted his whole bed, mosquito net and all, and brought him up to the dining hall. They pulled him through the line and they had his breakfast for him. He was just starting to wake up. He was having "breakfast in bed," and the cook came by with a big pitcher of water and said, "John, are you having a hard time waking up?" And John's like, "Uh, uh, I dunno," and then he saw the water and said, "Oh, yeah, I'm up, I'm up!" The cook said, "Let me just make sure." So he dumped the water all over him!

—*Lara, 15*

The other night I was sleeping in my bed and there was something crawling around my feet. And I was like, "What?" And I thought I knocked it out of my bed. And all of a sudden I felt it crawling up my arm and down my neck. So I went crazy, and I saw this thing crawling along my pillow. My roommate was sitting there laughing hysterically, and I was going crazy! I finally got myself out of bed 'cause I was caught in the blankets, and I threw it off the bed. It was, like, this big moth! I was going crazy, 'cause one of the wings had broken, so the houseparent came in and he killed it for me. It was so funny!

—Meredith, 13

There's a Japanese kid named Ken, he comes from Tokyo, Japan. He came in not knowing any English. It was really funny how he teaches us Japanese and we teach him to speak English. For example, one time we asked him, "How do you say 'peace'?"
And he said, "Peace?"
We said, "Yes, peace."
He said, "In Japanese?"
We said, "Yes, in Japanese."
He said, "Peace is peace."
We said, "Peace is peace?"

He said, "Yeah, peace is peace."
We said, "How do you say 'war'?"
"Peace."
"No," we said, "how do you say 'war'?"
He said, "War? In Japanese?"
We said, "Yeah."
He said, "Peace."

—Jason, 14½

Me and a friend of mine were going up to get some hot water for tea and we didn't know how to work the machine. So we started pushing all the buttons on there, 'cause we figured one of them would have to start it. All of a sudden it starts making all these noises and coffee starts pouring out all over the place. We ran and got another pitcher and we were holding it there. Suddenly it stopped and then water started squirting out the other one. We finally got a thing of water and it finally stopped.

—Chad, 14

One of the funniest things that ever happened to me at camp was when a friend of mine named Lukeman was leaning his elbow against my leg and we were both sitting down. He had his face pressed against his fist and his elbow against my knee and he thought that my knee was his and he kept poking at my knee. Suddenly he looked up and said, "Dang! I can't feel nothing in my leg!"

—Jason, 14½

For an acting class we had to sit somewhere that we have never sat before and observe our environment. So I sat in the closet, and I was observing my environment, and my friend Betsy came in and asked me what I was doing while I was trying to observe. She started hanging on the coat bar, and she was playing with these little curtain hooks we have, and she was playing hockey with them going, "Goal!

Goal!'' So it was very hard to concentrate for fifteen minutes. If I flunk acting class that's her fault.

—Tory, 13

Lights Out!

"Cabin Five has got to be the noisiest. . . ."

We have taps, and that means that we have to turn all the lights off. And after taps we get to have flashlights for fifteen minutes maybe, it depends on how nice the counselor is. Sometimes we're really tired, that's when we fall asleep right away. But usually we talk for awhile, and we get really into talking, and we start laughing at everything. Then the counselors come in and start yelling at us. Then we're quiet again. Then someone just whispers and when they whisper, then they start talking, then they get louder and louder and louder again. And see, sometimes townies come in from across the lake, like last night they walked by our bunk and everyone was getting really scared. That's why everyone was talking most of the time last night.

—Tammy, 9½

Every night there's this duck. It's been quacking its head off all week. It seems like it's a duck crying for its mother, and it's from the lake. The first night, we didn't know what it was, and we got so scared that we were up till, like, one o'clock saying, "What was that? What was that?" We thought it was a rat or something.

—*Debbie, 10*

The only thing that I can't really stand about it is the kid next to me can't seem to keep quiet. All the counselors have to speak to her and when she finally falls asleep, we can all fall asleep.

—*Lauren, 10½*

When the lights are out, it gets really spooky, because you think you see different things. Your imagination runs wild!

—*Kim, 10*

Some nights we have this thing called reflections. After everybody turns off the lights, we pick one topic—sometimes it's like the scariest thing that ever happened to you, or the funniest thing that ever happened—and everybody tells about it. And it always ends up that we're always talking about boys.

—Sarah, 13

I like lights out because it's fun to play with your flashlight and move your flashlight all around and make somebody disco in the middle (it looks like it's slow motion). But when the flashlights have to go out, sometimes my eyes start to hurt, 'cause you're used to having a little bit of light on. It's just sometimes scary.

—Debbie, 10½

When lights are off I get wormy. Sometimes I like hearin' scary stories to make me fall asleep and make me feel scared.

—Lee, 10

After the lights go out in my cabin, we start whispering. I walk over to Dan's bed (he's another kid in my cabin), and we start talkin'. We start whispering, start foolin' around. Then once in a while, we'll say something funny and we'll both start laughing out loud and someone will come over to our cabin and say, "Be quiet in there!" It just keeps going—the same pattern pretty much—and every now and then, someone turns the overhead lights on, and outside people are sayin', "Lights out!" Then every once in a while, someone will come up to the window and someone inside our cabin will say, "Lights out, dork!" to the person outside. One night, a car came up, and a kid in our cabin yelled as loud as he can, "Lights out, dork!" and immediately the lights in the car went out.

—Alex, 12

I get kinda nervous, 'cause every time the lights are out I can't see what I'm doin'. It's very dark. Sometimes I fall off the bed. I don't know what I'm doin'.

—Jeffrey, 10

The first night we came here, me and my friend Christine stayed up the whole night! Like, we'd go to sleep and then we'd wake each other up 'cause we were bored. We kept everybody up in our cabin, and we kept gettin' in trouble.

—Anna, 11

I think when the lights go out it's the most exciting part. Cabin Five has got to be the noisiest (that's the cabin we're in), the noisiest cabin after dark, because we talk, and we have M & M fights, and cheeseball fights, and everything.

—Ina, 12

I sleep on the bottom bunk, and right over me there's this kid who snores so loud that everyone wakes up in the cabin. He snores all night; it's really annoying.

—Michael, 13

Once, when our normal counselor was away, we had another counselor. In the middle of the night he was having a nightmare and screamed, "Help, help! Save me!" and I was so tired that I thought it was part of *my* dream. When the other kids got up and said, "Are you all right?" I thought that they were responding to my dream. But in the morning they explained what happened: he had a dream and thought a monster was pulling him under our cabin.

—Daniel, 12

The Scariest Thing

"Everyone, where are you?!"

Last year I was in Donald's cabin, and we went on an overnight. We wanted to start a fire to cook some hot dogs and we didn't have any matches, so Donald, the counselor, had to leave to get some matches, and he took two kids. So we was sittin' there in the dark, and one kid started tellin' *Friday the 13th* stories. After that we went and sat in the place we were supposed to sleep. The camp dog followed us, and we didn't know it. He kept on walkin' around in the woods, and some kid kept on talkin' about a bear. Then Donald came back and we didn't know it was Donald. All we saw was this person. We kept on saying, "Donald, is that you?" and he wouldn't answer, and we all screamed! Then he said, "OK, it's me!" and then he lit the match and we sat at the fire.

—Doug, 12

Sometimes when I wake up late at night and I have to go to the bathroom, I feel scared to go down there by myself. Sometimes I see shadows in the night 'n stuff; that's why I don't like to go by myself. That's the scariest part about camp; you don't have nobody to go with to the bathroom. They're all busy sleeping.

—*Marshee, 11*

A couple of counselors got together a program called "Lore of the Gore," and it's like a very exclusive club that you have to go through an initiation for. Last month, what they did for initiation was, at about eleven-thirty at night, they'd come around to your living unit, and we all got together and we had to climb for about forty-five minutes up the side of a mountain in the dark with flashlights, all close together. This was so we wouldn't lose anybody. When we got there, we didn't know what the initiation was gonna be. So they put us in tents and they said, "Okay, we'll come get you." So they'd get you, and then they'd blindfold you, and you'd have to walk around on the side of a mountain, not on paths, like through rocks and everything. You were climbing down, like doing rock-climbing, with a blindfold on, in the dark, with somebody leading you around and you don't know what they're going to do to you.

—*Lara, 15*

When I was going to the bathroom, I saw an animal that was comin' towards me. It was a rabbit, but I didn't know what it was. I had my flashlight starin' at him, his eye was turnin' green, so I ran back to the cabin.

—*Hayden, 13*

It's scary when we have our free swim and they blow three whistles; that means something's wrong. A couple of days ago they blew three whistles and we thought somebody was missing, but it was only a test.

—*Michelle, 9*

One time me and my friend were out in a paddleboat, and we were just paddlin' around, and we stopped for a little bit. We looked down in the water, and we saw this snapping turtle as big as the paddleboat swimming under the boat, and he just kept swimming around and around the boat. So, all of a sudden, we just put on the speed and beat it out of there before we got hit!

— *Steven, 13*

At night, after the activity, I was walking, and there's like a little path that leads to our bunk. I thought, "Everybody's behind me," and I was just walking there, and no one was behind me! I was so scared. Then I got paranoid. I thought everyone was moving and gonna grab me. It was like, "Everyone, where are you?" It was my imagination, 'cause the wind was blowing, and the trees were rustling, and I was so scared.

— *Debbie, 13*

We were coming back from a campfire, going to our cabins, and at the campfire we had been listening to ghost stories. And I went on the wrong path, and I went through the woods, and I couldn't find my way back. It was really dark and I was really scared. Then a kid jumped out and said, "Boo!" So I got angry at him and I hit him. I was horrified the rest of the night.

—*Daniel, 12*

Going Home

". . . I hope I can come back."

If you're here for the whole summer, the last session is really the worst because you really got close to the kids that were here at camp. By the end you're afraid you're just gonna leave, and you're never going to see them again, and you're not really going to be able to keep in touch. Last year and the year before I had these favorite counselors, and this year I have a favorite counselor too. Last year my favorite counselor was moving to Albuquerque, and I was gonna miss her 'cause I would never see her again. We gave each other our addresses and it was really sad. When the bus comes (we have a bus from the YMCA to the camp), and when you see all the campers get on the bus, you see everyone crying — so it makes it real sad.

—Joelle, 11

This is my fifth year back, so I sort of got used to saying good-bye, but you never get completely used to it. We have the candlelight ceremony the last night of camp, but you don't leave on a sad note 'cause the next day we have a horse show. Whether you win or lose, you have a lot of fun. People just sort of slip away with their parents. You don't really have a "hugging formal good-bye" ceremony, so it's a little bit easier.

— Debbie, 14

On Friday night, around seven or eight o'clock, we go down to our waterfront, which is down the hill. The counselors get a cup and they get a candle, and we take them down to the water, and we sing songs and we have a campfire. Each cabin lights a candle, and we set them all into the lake, and we make a wish — like someone wishes, "I hope I see other people," and "I hope I can come back."

— Anna, 11

I always stay for the whole summer. At the end of camp you always have the final banquet. They have this whole big spread of food, and everyone's crying, and nobody wants to leave the camp. And everyone is taking pictures and taking addresses and phone numbers and everything.

When you go to bed you don't really go to bed — you practically stay up all night talking to your friends and everything. The counselors don't really care, 'cause it's the last day. They sit up and talk to you too. The section director comes in and he talks to you and says good-bye. The next morning is really a madhouse, 'cause you have to get everything packed up and ready to get on the bus. When you get to the bus stop, everybody is crying and everything. It's really depressing.

— Bunkie, 11

The reason I like going home is because it's, like, so homey, and you get in your own bed, and you got your own TV. You can drink milk or something anytime you want, or play with your dog. It's just fun!

— Billy, 13

When you're getting ready to go home you get up, pack everything, and then you wonder, "I wonder if my mother got a new haircut or something and if I'm going to recognize her. Has anything changed since I've been gone?" At the end people don't want to leave. You have bad times, like at one point you want to go home so badly you'll do anything for it. After you get home you start thinking, "Did I have more good times than I did bad times?" You usually have more good times than bad times. That's why I like camp.

—*Paul, 12*

The ride home is the worst. You've got cross feelings. You're happy to be going home and being with your parents, or sad to be leaving. You're getting into the car after crying your eyes out, and you're so happy to be seeing your parents. I personally just babble on about everything that's been happening. I try to fit, in this case, two months into about two hours.

—*Lara, 15*

I always have—I don't know why, I mean, I doubt it would ever happen—but I always have this terrible feeling that no one's going to show up and pick me up. I mean, I know that I could get home, and I know people where I could get dropped off and everything, but I always have the feeling that nobody's going to pick me up or something's happened to someone I know. That's pretty scary.

—*Charlie, 13*

Sometimes you miss being at home when you're at camp, and when you're at home you miss camp. You wake up early expectin' to go and raise the flag.

—Dean, 14

When you're first driving home, and you go down your street, and you're going to see your house, it's really weird. It's different. It's like a different location. It's so weird to go home from a bunk to a nice house and everything. When you come into your house it's nice that you're in a house, and you can have real food and see your own bed.

—Michelle, 13

A couple of years ago, when I first came to camp, I used to cry 'cause I really didn't want to leave. The reason why I cried was 'cause I wasn't coming back up, because my mother wasn't sure if I could handle a month here, but now I can handle it, and she signed me up for two months at a time. I really do like this place, and I'll always come here until, maybe, if I get a good recommendation from my counselor, I could work here!

—John, 13

When I left camp last year I was crying. I mean, I like this camp so much, and I just couldn't stop thinking about it for about half the school year. I thought about it a little less as I got more involved in school, but you know, I just kept thinking back. Then, before I came to camp, like the month before I came here, I was really nervous—not that I wouldn't like the people or anything, because I knew I'd like 'em; I knew that a lot of my friends would be back—but that it would have changed, you know, because I like the camp as it was, and I didn't really want it to change all that much. I always dreamed what would happen when I got to camp, you know. Like last year, when I came to camp, I didn't know what I was doing. I just came over and they said, "Go over there and sign up at the desk," and so I come over to this lady and she says, "Oh jolly good, you're in Cabin One," and I was thinking, "This is a pretty weird place," but, you know, before I came this year, I was thinking, "Oh boy, I can't wait to hear Maggie say, "Oh jolly good, you're in Cabin Two."

—*Josh, 11*

Autographs

Autographs

Autographs

Autographs

Write Your Own Camp Adventure Here

Write Your Own Camp Adventure Here

Write Your Own Camp Adventure Here

Write Your Own Camp Adventure Here